TIM JONAS

HOW STRANGE THE WAYS

OF HEALING ARE...

Hetty Overeem

Copyright © 2010 by Hetty Overeem

TIM JONAS
by Hetty Overeem

Printed in the United States of America

ISBN 9781615799572

Unless otherwise indicated, Bible quotations are taken from the New International Version of the Bible, Copyright © 1973, 1978, 1984 by International Bible Society (This edition 1982).

www.xulonpress.com

For all those who feel they're perilously balancing on the tight-rope of life, whereas others just (seem to) walk happily along; those to whom healing seems far away.
Don't give up – *God* doesn't!

« **I am who I am.** » (Exodus 3, 14)

Acknowledgments

Warm thanks to Alice Goodman and Robert Mattmann for their support, advice and corrections; Kate Harper; and Madeleine Anaya - Stämpfli, who started it all by passing me my very first book on inner healing !

And thank God for signposts like Dr. Atef, Karl Barth, Jan Karon, C. S. Lewis, Eugene H. Peterson ('The Message'), Adrian Plass, Phil Schmidt, Teo van der Weele and John White ('The Archives Of Anthropos'). They all pointed to the only one who has a right to the title of « Truthcarrier » (chapter 8), and so they urged me on.

INTRODUCTION

Tim Jonas is one of these people who have lost their faith in God because of « things that happened »… He leads his ordinary life, neither unhappy nor happy, until a « guide » intervenes and invites him to go through the events of his life – but not alone this time!

In a strange world where fiction mingles with reality, Tim learns that he doesn't have to run away from his fears any more, that he can face them with this very special guide at his side.

He discovers that healing *is* possible, even if it is slow, and that the longest way round – the real Tim discovering real life with a real God – is not the most comfortable, but truly the shortest way home.

This book started when I discovered how often all of us are imprisoned in distorted images…of ourselves, of God, of others.

To be honest, I got angry, *so* angry with these caricatures which seem to wrap themselves around us - and God - like so many sticky spiderwebs, preventing us from becoming our real selves in Jesus Christ.

Of course God, being totally free and totally himself, cannot be imprisoned in these images (the Bible calls them idols), but he suffers as much as we do from our habit of looking at him, at ourselves and at others in this hazy and distorted way. So he gets to work and, having sent his Son to set things right in the center, sends his Spirit to do the necessary job of cleaning up the rest. And the Spirit uses ordinary people to help him. Strange, but then, that's how it is. That's how *he* is!

Following him around on the surprising paths of healing he takes, I just love to see how deeply wounded people can get back on their feet again.

Most of Tim's experiences reflect the stories of people I counseled, especially those of abused women and men.

Table of contents

1) MEETING

My name is Tim. Tim Jonas. No, not Jones - Jonas. I know it's a funny name but then, it's mine.

I'm a grown man. At least, that's what people say. Nowadays I'm not so sure, but I remember I was sure before, before I met this man, this fellow who was to be my companion during the strange days that followed. I can still hear his voice, his first words of greeting when I saw him: « Blessed are you among men! »

Now I don't know about you but I have some vague knowledge of the Bible, and these words strongly reminded me of what someone said to Mary.*

« Nice, » I said to myself, « but out of place. I'm not Mary and as far as I can tell, I'm not particularly blessed either. »

But there he was, his hand outstretched, a smile in his eyes.

It was on a sunny day in late August that I met him, or maybe I should say, that he met me. In fact, it was not so much meeting each other as my gradually realizing that I was not alone.

I'm quite easily frightened, and you will surely agree with me that there's something unnerving about walking through a forest, deep in thought, while slowly becoming aware that somebody's been walking beside you all along - or at least for quite a bit of time. But, strangely enough, I wasn't frightened. The person walking beside me seemed to fit in somehow, to fit in with my thoughts, with this peaceful forest glade and this particularly beautiful summer day. Indeed, the sun had a special quality today as it showered its glittering light lavishly on the rustling leaves, making their colours bright and clear without getting aggressive. And I myself? Well, you know this funny feeling, when you've seen a good film, or read a good book; you've been completely absorbed in the story, but now it has come to an end, and you trundle back into dreary reality with a feeling of loss and regret.

It was a bit like that, but the other way round. It felt like walking from one world into another, quietly sliding from dry, down-to-earth routine reality into something new and colourful and unexpected, where anything could happen. Like suddenly realizing you had company...

« Hi, » I said tentatively. Not very inventive, I agree, but I don't know how to address complete strangers who somehow don't seem to be complete strangers, and this was as good a beginning as any. At least I couldn't do much wrong.

« Blessed are you among men! So now you can see me? »

I shook his outstretched hand. « Well... yes. Yes, I do see you. Does that mean that you've been here all along? »

« You could say so, » he admitted, « but I'm glad you finally realized I'm here, for that makes it a lot easier for me to teach you to see and to show you the way. Would you like me to? »

I pondered over this strange question with a bit of irritation. What was he talking about?

Teach me to see? Of all the superior things to say! Whom did he think he was talking to, a mere child? Curiosity and reluctance battled in me. Reluctance won. I heard myself say, « I don't think so. You know, I'm quite a loner, and I believe my eyes are all right, thank you. »

I turned to be on my way, but he stopped me. « And where will you go then? »

I hesitated. Yes, where would I go? To be honest, I didn't have the faintest idea. It seemed to me I had been going on for a long time, forever on some unknown errand, urged on by... by what? Something telling me that I had to go on to find the thing I most wanted, the one thing that would make life worth living?

« You see, » he said, looking at me intently, « that's why I'm here. To help you find what you're seeking. You can't, you know. Not on your own. But you don't have to because I'm your guide. I like to show people the way, that's what guides are for. Will you accept me ? »

I felt a bit silly. Me, a grown man (now, why do I insist?), needing the help of some weird guide… At the same time, a sense of urgency came over me. This was important. This moment was important: a moment not to let slip through my fingers. What was more, had I not thought right up to that moment that I was seeing perfectly clearly, only to find out that someone had been walking beside me, someone whom I'd definitely never seen before?

To my own surprise I suddenly discovered that I wanted very much to be shown the way, whatever that might mean. Me, independent old Tim, I suddenly wanted to know what it was to be guided and led. So I answered, « Yes. Yes, I will. »

And I fleetingly wondered why I felt so much at peace.

*Luke 1, 42   *****

2) DISCOVERING

« Come, » he said, and then, pointing upwards, « That's where we go. »

We climbed up the hill through a kind of ditch, probably the bed of a dried-up stream. The sunlight was very beautiful here. It produced endless varieties of green, mingled with splashes of gold that appeared and vanished with the sighs of the wind through the leaves.

Then I heard the sound of rushing water, soft at first, but gradually louder, until we reached a clearing from which I could see a waterfall.

The water was tumbling down from sheer grey rocks, splashing onto big boulders, black and brown and a deep red, joyously dancing with the ferns that reached out to meet it, catching the sunlight, searching and finding its way through a multitude of smaller, copper-coloured pebbles, to continue flowing with a contented murmur through the grass which was littered with fat, yellow buttercups. The effect was strikingly beautiful.

I was just reflecting that the time for buttercups was normally gone when my companion said: « This is it. Go in. »

« Go in? » I echoed stupidly.

« In, yes. Undress, then stand under the waterfall. It is mine, and very special. It will give you what you're longing for, and you will find rest, and new life. Will you not go in? »

I did as he told me, I don't really know why. Maybe it was the surprising authority with which my new companion spoke. Maybe it was the inviting quality of the waterfall itself. Maybe it was the impression of utter reality presenting itself to me, asking to be taken, and held, and enjoyed. Maybe it was just my own, deep, aching longing for something that was different, not just a copy of something else, but the thing itself. Maybe it was all of that, but anyway, I slowly undressed and went in.

It was - how to describe it? The water had a peculiar texture, more solid, as it were, than water normally is. Despite this quality, it felt smooth to the touch, and it was quite warm. But most of all, it was the most waterlike water I'd ever touched, and I'll ever touch, in my life. I'm sorry if this sounds silly, I just can't describe it otherwise. It was as if it took me into itself, letting me share its movement of dancing, turning, whirling, leaping, mingling with the light, singing its song…

Yes, that was it ! It had its own, beautiful, crystal-clear song, and once I was inside the water I found myself singing too, quite naturally, and the singing made me even more aware of the water's unique « realness ».

But what astonished me most was that, apart from a strange, quiet certainty that somehow all was well, I had no particular, extraordinary feelings. It was not necessary. It was not expected from me.

« Will you remember the waterfall? » he asked.

Of course I would. How could I ever forget? I felt its song would forever accompany me.

« Will you really remember? » he insisted. « Have another look. This water is the Original, the Source of all Reality. Will you be able to distinguish it from the unreliable copies, or even the caricatures that are bound to show up? There are so many of them, and if you are not careful you will mix them up with the real thing. »

I nodded. « I think I will recognize it. It's different from anything I know. But anyway, will you not be there to remind me? »

« Yes, I will; but from time to time my image will grow dimmer and so will the image of the waterfall. Remember its colours. Remember the way it moves, remember its dance and its song. Remember! »

*****

3) GETTING LOST

After quite a bit of walking we came to a field full of flowers. I could only stare when we approached it. There were just so many of them, and the colours of some of them were so bright and so lovely they literally took my breath away. Others were not as beautiful, but even they held me as if in a spell. With glazed eyes I stepped into the field.

« Stop! » said the guide. « You can go in, but you have to take the path, or you'll get lost. »

I didn't heed the warning. Wasn't this what I had been waiting for and what the waterfall had suggested? This glorious, splendid feast of colour and intensity, of brightness and stillness, of highest majesty and smallest treasure… it was too much. I said haltingly, « If seeing the waterfall does this to me, why, it was powerful indeed! ». And I headed for the weaving stalks and flowers.

« Stop! » repeated my companion, sharply this time. « You're not used to this! Wait until I show you the path! »

But this time I didn't want him to show me the way. What path was there to show, anyway? With the whole of paradise before me? I laughed happily and went in.

Immediately I was engulfed by scents, and the colours were dancing before my eyes. It felt like being in a whirlpool, a bit frightening, but wonderful. I held my hands outstretched in front of me like a sleepwalker, and so I went, from one flower to another, to another and another...

Suddenly I tripped over a hidden branch and fell flat on my face. I wanted to pick myself up and be on my way when I suddenly found myself looking at a tiny, rather ugly flower that I would not have seen had I not stumbled. It had a grey-brown heart surrounded by yellow petals and looked quite ordinary, but as I continued to examine it, a queer sensation took hold of me. It was as if this little heart were sucking myself into it, as if I were still falling, not on solid earth now, but into an endless space. And then I realized with a shock that that was exactly what was happening. I was falling.

Afraid now, I started to struggle and find some hold, but there was none. Relentlessly, the flower was drawing me into itself. Deeper and deeper I sank until I felt I would forever be falling, falling, until the end of my life. I was getting so tired I couldn't resist the pull anymore, and I was just thinking of giving up altogether when a voice called my name and a hand grabbed my shoulder, turning me round, lifting me up, tearing me away from the bottomless hole, pulling, drawing, fighting the surge of the tiny flower's all-engulfing strength. I was helplessly floating, but up I went, and up, until I saw the blue sky again. At last I found myself lying on the ground, gulping for breath, shaking all over and crying like a baby.

When I finally looked up, I saw my companion sitting beside me, lost in thought, or so it seemed.

« Beware, » he said after a while, turning to me. « These places are far too dangerous for roaming on your own. »

I remained in silence for a while, but too many questions were boiling in my head.

« What happened? » I blurted out, trying to get back up on my unsteady feet.

« You got too near the flower of fascination, » was the answer. « You could have lost yourself completely there. »

« Was it you who called me back? » I asked, thinking of the saving voice and hand.

He nodded.

« Thanks, » I said, trying to sound grateful, but still feeling shocked and strangely angry.

« Why do these stupid flowers grow here ? They're a public danger! »

He shrugged his shoulders. « That's a difficult question, and I can't even begin answering it right now. Let's just say for the moment that they exist, and that we should start from that fact. Are you ready to go on? »

« No, » I said sulkingly. « Why does the waterfall give you the impression that everything is more alive and then, when you think you can grasp a part of it, it turns out to be a fake. It's unfair. »

My friend looked at me quizzically. « It's not a fake, you know, but these flowers are not there to be picked carelessly. They're specially designed for being given... and received. »

We ended up walking around this field he told me was called the field of feelings, and he showed me some very particular specimen. « They tend to take your perspective away, if you let them, » he continued. « When that happens they take up all the space, so that you don't see the waterfall any more. And strange as it may sound, this taking all the space spoils their beauty and hides their truth. »

I didn't answer for the simple reason that I didn't know what to say.

« Look at this. » He suddenly stopped and pointed at a peculiar dark brown plant. « You may look at it, but only from a safe distance. »

I craned my neck to see the plant, and immediately a sudden panic took hold of me. The thing was awful. It was so big, no plant had the right to be as big as that. What's more, to be there at all. Or was it me who had no right to be there at all? It was overwhelming. It made me want to vomit and, oh horror, I had the same feeling of being sucked up all over again.

« No, » said my guide, « you're not going to fall. Stay with me. » He threw an arm around my shoulders. « But do you see what happens? This one is called the plant of fear. It can grow into one of the most ugly things that exist. But then, it can be useful, too, so you must learn to recognize it in its different shapes, in order not to get hurt too much by it. »

« Fear, » I said shakily. « So that's its name. It is horrible, it is sneaky, it's sticky, it's so *strong*… But it is different from the first one. What did you say its name was? »

« The flower of fascination, » he repeated. « Actually that one is a sort of parasite, it can wind itself around any flower, strangling its character. And when it gets strong enough, it will transfer some of its own qualities to the flower, for instance the sucking force you experienced. Very dangerous. A shame, really. »

He gave me a wink. « But now that you've fallen into one yourself, you'll surely be able to recognize it the next time! So avoid it by all means. »

****

4) GIVING AND TAKING

« W hat did you mean exactly when you said the flowers were designed to be given and received? » I asked while we were walking alongside a broad, calmly flowing stream. « Who does the giving? »

« The Giver, » was the answer.

This was not very helpful, so I tried again. « Who is he, then? Do you know him? Personally I mean? »

« Personally, yes », he nodded, and I detected a gleam in his eye. « Actually, we are very close, and we see quite a bit of each other. He's the landowner, so to speak, and all three of us together are seeing to it that this property is well taken care of. »

« All three? There's yet another one of you around then? »

« Oh yes, you're going to meet him soon. The Landlord himself, too ».

« Why is he called the Giver? »

« Because it describes him so well. Actually, he has other names, but I like this one. It means he is the one real Giver, you know. The Original. Remember what I said about the waterfall? The Original of all givers, of all giving. »

I thought I understood, and said so. « The giver of all good things? »

« Yes, of course », he answered. « But more than that. Above all, he is the Giver of himself. He wants to share his own being, his personality. He wants to enter people's hearts or, if you prefer, to take people into his own heart. »

I definitely didn't prefer this, the memory of the flower still being very vivid in my mind.

He seemed to read my thoughts. « No, it's not like that, » he reassured me. « In fact, nothing could be more different, but I see it happen all the time; people meet a bad copy of something, and it thoroughly disgusts them. Then, when they meet the real thing, they remember the fake. And if they haven't learned to distinguish between the two, they'll throw both of them out. Or they'll take both of them in, which isn't much better. »

I tried to make sense of this. « You mean this Giver has a way of giving himself to people without losing himself, and of receiving them without becoming either dependent or possessive? »

« Well yes, » he laughed. « That's a quite a good description! »

We walked for a while in silence.

Then another thought came to my mind. « Is that not what the word 'spirit' means? A part of this Giver being in us, so to say? »

« That definition would be too passive, » he said, « too rigid for my taste. You can't expect him to be put into your pocket - or into any place for that matter, where he would stay, like a sort of domestic, tame being. Nor would I, by the way! Why, he's more like a movement, » he continued, warming to his subject, « he's even the first movement, the Original of all movements:

The Giver gives himself to you. He comes to you like a breeze, caressing you, enfolding you… He will leave his mark on you, but you can't capture him, no, never… »

Something weird happened. While my friend was talking, I felt as if this very movement he was describing touched me, lifted me up, enfolded me just for a moment... Then it was gone again, leaving a curious, aching longing in my heart.

« So many people try to capture him, » he said, rather sadly I thought. « They don't want to lose so precious a gift, so they try to shut him up in whatever prison comes in handy; a cathedral, or a religious experience, a doctrine, or an image... They think they can control him then, but when they come looking for their treasure there are just walls around nothing. »

After a short silence he went on, «You can only receive him. Ask for him and receive him. So easy. And so difficult. »

I thought I saw what he meant. In a way, this fleeting movement had been a terrifying experience. « It feels so ... so fragile, so vulnerable. It's a little bit like letting go of a saving hand... »

I saw he understood. « It is, » he nodded, « but *this* saving hand will definitely not let you go! That's what living out of a promise means. »

« Seems awfully risky to me. How can I be sure that this Giver will come to me again? »

He smiled. « Don't worry, he will! It will be different next time, not because he changes, but because you do. But come he will. In a way he never even really leaves, for he's as close to you as I am now, but we will talk about that later. For the moment I just want you to store in your heart all that happens to you here, a bit like pieces of a puzzle. Later you can take these pieces out, one by one. You can look at them, put them together, and so begin to see the picture. It's the way to become free ».

« Free?! You mean I'm not free now? »

« Are you? »

He stopped, looked around, saw a boulder and sat down, his hand patting the one next to it.

« Sit down. This will take some time! »

*****

5) GETTING FREE

I was glad of the halt. Waterfall, field and flowers, fascinating or not, had been just about enough for my senses and needed some quiet ruminating.

« Freedom, » began my guide, « is to the Giver what intensity is to the waterfall; they belong together. You cannot come closer to the Giver without getting a little bit freer yourself, and without longing to be freer yet. Yes, longing is so important… The longing for freedom draws it nearer, and it is one of the gifts the Giver likes to give first, because it teaches us to ask.

Now, freedom… Freedom is the direction we're taking. It's the place we're heading for, but also the path we're taking. It's the perspective, but also the walking itself. ».

It sounded all right but a bit abstract for my taste. « What about concrete things to do, or not to do, in order to get nearer to it? »

« Concrete things, » my guide mused. « Yes, of course they are there, too. But let's put first things first. You see, first of all you need to hear the Giver's call in order to know the longing. Then you need to receive; to know that he has given, is giving and will give. You need to receive him deep in your heart and know him there, know that he is good. Otherwise you cannot love him. Otherwise you will fear him, and he wants to drive out your fear. He wants you to know him as he really is; for he is who he is. »

« Ah yes, Exodus something*, » I said lamely. « Says about the same. »

I had never got on well with those particular words. Somehow they made this God of the Bible look a trifle tyrannic. Who am I? Joke coming: who I am...! As if he wanted to disguise himself, to avoid nearer contact.

Again I had the impression that the guide was reading my thoughts.

« I didn't want to sound evasive, that's not my style. What would be the point, especially here? No, what I meant is that he is just utterly true to himself, to his character. What he is, he is with his whole heart, totally, until the end. If he says he's faithful, well, then he is. And he will show himself as such. He always does. »

My head was getting dizzy. « And... what about freedom? »

« Yes, it seems like I'm going the long way round, doesn't it? » he said cheerfully. « But it's part of the answer to your question about what things you have to do or not to do, in order to become free. As I said before, the road *to* freedom is always the road *of* freedom. It is impossible to say, 'Now that's it. Here's where I am and here's where I'm going to stay,' because it's a question of always following that same movement we were talking about. In fact, it is more a movement toward freedom than a road. »

« Freedom from what? »

« What would you say? » he asked with a glint in his eyes.

« I don't know really. I can think of lists. Bible lists, or church lists, I'm not very well acquainted with either. Things like greed, and lust, and hate... jealousy, anger, egoism... but... » I faltered.

« Yes? » he urged me on.

« Well, these lists always give me a queer sensation. Kind of unworldly... Not being in touch with good old reality any more, if you know what I mean. I try to imagine a person being free from those things, and all I come up with is somebody rather insipid, and unhealthily pious, a person I'd rather avoid than talk to... »

I looked at him askance, surely this was not a very successful remark... But my friend laughed.

« I'm not surprised! »

« Do you mean we don't have to become, er, free then? But you said... »

« I was talking about getting free, not quitting reality, » he corrected. « I'd like you to meet the Landlord's son. He's not what I would call insipid... No, what you have in mind is the bad copy again, or even the caricature. I'm sorry if I seem to be harping on that, but it is necessary. For it is what you people call a leitmotiv; it keeps coming back, in endless variations. But the leitmotiv can be nice, whereas the caricature never is... You see, the Landlord has his enemies, too. And one in particular. As soon as an Original comes out, this enemy makes enough bad copies to scatter them all over the place. He never gets tired of it. »

« I wonder why your famous Landlord doesn't get tired of it, » I said a little bit grudgingly.

« Oh, he does. But he doesn't stop him. Not yet. He contents himself with trying to get people back to the Original, making them so fed up with the fake they just start panting for the real stuff. So, talking about freedom... »

« Ah yes, that's where we were! »

« Freedom is just utterly wonderful. It's like the freedom of the bird to sing, the freedom of the happy dog to leap and chase a rabbit or catch a snowball, just for the fun of it. It's the freedom of the writer to think and discover and smile and write down what feels right. It's the freedom of the composer to hear, somewhere in his head, the beginnings of a tune; to turn it round and round and model it and be modeled by it, and to let it come out as a beautiful whole... It's the freedom of the child to play and laugh and get dirty and be cleaned and get dirty again... It's the freedom to LIVE. »

I felt that things, instead of getting clearer, were becoming more and more confusing.

« Yes but… it's all very well, but I still don't know what to do… » It sounded a bit plaintive but I couldn't help it.

Again he laughed. « Don't you see? Freedom consists of getting nearer to him. Being guided by him, by me, by his son. It's not just doing what you want… nor what you don't want, for that matter, » he added hastily, seeing my face. « Freedom means following the call of goodness because you've discovered, or maybe just guessed, what real goodness is. Once you've tasted a little bit of the Original, you'll go for more. You just follow your own thirst! And once you're on your way, you discover that some things help you and urge you on - whereas others will slow you down, make you stumble or fall, or lose your way altogether. So the real question is, what do you choose?! »

* Exodus 3, 14   *****

6) DREAMING

That night I had a dream. A strange and not very nice one.

I lay on a bed in a large room with high walls, trying to get some sleep. But I could not sleep as long as this horrible swarm of flies was there, hanging in thick clusters from the ceiling, flying round in circles and crawling in my bed.

Finally I couldn't stand it any more. I got up, opened the window and chased the swarm away. Yes! Off they went, flying out of the window. I think I left it open afterwards.

I got into bed again, but, oh no, lots and lots of them were still around, creeping, crawling - no sleep for me that night, no way.

Then a woman came and took my pillow into her hands.

« You see, this is where they came from, » she said. « This is their source ». And she started to tear the pillow-case apart.

I stopped her, shouting, « Don't! I've got nothing else to lay my head on. »

« It has to be washed », she insisted. But I didn't want to let go.

I told my friend about the dream.

« Yes, » he said thoughtfully, « very true. »

« What is very true? »

« Tell me first, what do you make of it yourself? »

I shrugged my shoulders. « I wondered about this having nothing else to lay my head on. Does that mean, on what foundation do I build my life? And the head, does that stand for rational thinking? Or for memories? I really don't know. Do you? And what about the flies? »

He nodded. « I'll give you a hint, and then let it just stew for a bit, okay? Their name should help you. They are called *Bitterflies*. »

*****

7) TAKING TIME

Suddenly my attention was attracted by a very strange spectacle. About thirty yards from where we were sitting a huge black panther was lying in the grass, watching its prey, whatever this was, with fierce eyes. Slowly it got up and approached its victim cautiously. Then suddenly, with outstretched claws, it jumped. I heard a muffled cry, and soon afterwards the beast came out of the bushes, dragging a furiously protesting bundle along.

I gasped. « It's… it's a human being! » I struggled to my feet and made for the animal. I don't know what I would have done, I didn't even have a stick to fight with, but my friend stopped me.

« Don't interfere, » he said. « You can't help. The animal won't kill him. Look. »

I stayed where I was, trembling.

Lazily the panther let go of its prey. The man, for that was what it was, lay still, watching the beast anxiously. And then began a show I'll never forget. I didn't know whether to laugh or to cry.

The panther lifted its paw and stood there, waiting expectantly. The man got up. The panther traced a circle in the sand. The man began to dance around his new master.

Then the animal started to talk. I couldn't really understand it, but apparently it was giving some new orders, in a rough, barking voice. The man obeyed perfectly, stood on his hands, walked on all fours, danced, clapping his hands furiously - he was totally at the big beast's beck and call. It was like being in a circus, only here the animal was clearly in charge of the human.

After a while, the panther seemed to get bored with its toy. It beckoned the man with its paw and took off in the direction of the forest. The man followed it as if he had a chain around his neck, faithfully, doggedly. I didn't see him again.

« Why didn't you interfere? » I asked my friend.

He didn't answer.

« Don't you care at all? » I flung at him.

He looked at me sadly. « I promise you, I do. I asked him again and again to resist. He could, you know. But he told me to go away. And I can't teach him how to resist if he doesn't want me for company. »

« But, » I protested, « you can help him now, can't you? You have power here. What will become of the poor chap now? »

« He will follow the beast. He will listen to it and obey its whims. He will not be happy, but he'll live. »

« What! It's even a question of life and death, and yet you didn't save him? What sort of a guardian are you? »

« I told you, he won't listen. Not for the moment anyway. Let him get thoroughly fed up with this stupid game. Maybe he'll call for me then. »

« And then? Will you help him? »

Now it was his turn to be angry. « Who do you think I am? Of course I will. True, I can't help him if he doesn't want me to help. Even I have to obey the rules of the land. But

I never, do you hear, never, ever, turn away from someone who calls me.

Look, over there. That's how it is supposed to work. »

I followed the direction of his pointing finger and saw another panther, as big as the first one, its coat the colour of silver. It followed a woman coming out of the forest, carrying some logs in its mouth and obediently dropping them where she told it to. Then they set out to work together, the beast fetching more wood from the forest, as the woman started to build some sort of a cabin.

« You see, that's what the Landlord intended, » said the guide. « The animals are there, in fact, everything in this country is there, to be used. Used respectfully, yes, by all means, but they are there to serve the humans, and not the other way round. »

A question rose in my mind. « Do they have a name, these animals? »

« Oh yes. There are a lot of different species, but they all spring from the same race. You know it, you have met it before. You call it « Time ».

*****

8) TRUTH HUNTING

It was a weird sight. Hundreds and hundreds of cardboard pieces hooked on wooden sticks, a whole forest of them. Some of them were just silently standing around, others were moving creakily as if a persistent wind were pushing them around. They all carried the same message written in huge letters:

FOLLOW ME!

When we came nearer, I saw that the things were alive. They all had what looked like big stocky arms with gnarly fingers, which the strange creatures used to point alternately to themselves and to some unknown destination further away. They were also saying things, but we were too far off to hear them clearly, especially as they were all talking at the same time.

« Strange, » I mused. « They all want you to follow them, but they all point in different directions. »

« Not surprising, » sighed my guide. « What you see here are looks, words, ideas and opinions. »

« Whose? »

« The people's. »

When he saw that I was waiting, he went on.

« They claim to be truthcarriers, and they are, for those stupid enough to believe them. In fact, they are truthbarriers. »

« But some carry the signature of very important people, » I protested, looking more closely at an inscription on the nearest one. « See, this one belongs to a famous politician, and over there … »

But my friend made an impatient gesture with his hand. « They're not reliable, » he said scornfully. « They're all right maybe, as long as they don't pretend to carry the truth. »

Now it was my turn to be sceptical. « The truth, » I said, with a little laugh that sounded a bit queer in my own ears, « the truth indeed! People either say it - or should I say he or she? - doesn't exist; or they heavily insist that it does, underlining equally heavily that they've got it all there nicely in their pocket. »

« Yes, » he said brightly. « That's why I said you can't trust people who claim to be truthcarriers. At the very best, you can become a signpost, but in that case you don't attract attention to yourself... You point to the only one who has a right to that title. Following him. Making up your mind what you honestly think is the truth, and trying to go in its wake as well as you can. »

I snorted. « Too dangerous! I've seen many people doing exactly that, sticking to what they - honestly! - think is the truth, fighting for it with all their might, wounding and killing all who are in their way. Or at least making life as miserable as possible for those who are not as enlightened as they believe themselves to be. »

He pondered for a while, then asked, « Why is it so? Either people don't want to look for the truth, ending up in an indifferent state of mind they call « neutrality » or a smug state of mind they call « tolerance », neither of which is real neutrality or real tolerance.

Or they look for the truth, not to follow it, but to capture it - you see, here we go again! - like one catches a bird with a net. But once they get hold of a little bit of truth and shut it away in their cage, it immediately gets lame, so to speak. It cannot be kept in a cage, it will just slowly die there. Or worse, it might turn into a ruthless, truthless monster. And when it escapes… beware! »

I listened to this speech with growing apprehension. I had reacted violently myself when confronted with the idea of truth, and well did I know why. But this didn't seem right either.

« Isn't there another way then? A better one? » I asked hesitatingly.

« Of course there is! » He looked at me. « Our way for instance! Looking for something real, solid, reliable, worth building upon. Looking for a path to go, a safe one, with the help of a guide such as me. Checking again and again whether you're still going in the same, chosen direction, to inner happiness. But to find that, you need to find the truth in person. Not the thing, not even the good thing. The person. »

« Strange, the way you talk. How could the truth become a person?! Anyway, your path doesn't seem a comfortable one to me, given the puzzle pieces I've seen so far!, » I said with feeling. « But why do you say inner happiness? Doesn't all happiness come from inside? »

« Heavens no! » he laughed. « With happiness it's the same as with nearly everything else; there's the Original and there are the fakes. Let's go back to the captured truths. They may look beautiful, they may even resemble the real truth, they may be ever so convincing, but when looked at closely they cannot hide what they really are, that is, poor imitations, fakes, caricatures. That's what always happens when things lose touch with their Designer. They get cut off and start to lead a life of their own, and that is their end. They are like those dead cardboard pieces busily pretending they are alive and reliable. The people who follow them lose themselves and may even end up sinking into the swamp of no light's land.

Now, with happiness it's the same. The Original is so beautiful, one of the masterpieces of the great Artist himself. Just looking at it takes your breath away. But it can only keep its beauty if you recognize the Artist's hand behind it, or maybe even better, if you see the Artist himself in the picture. Otherwise its brilliance fades away, it gets dark and sombre. The only thing left will be a frame holding an unrecognizeable picture consisting of just lines and dots. It won't make sense any more. »

« Aren't you a bit harsh? » I asked. « You seem to suggest that, outside of your Giver, or Artist, there's nothing left that's really worthwhile, in itself, I mean. »

« Is that harsh? » he asked, an astonished look in his eyes. « It seems only logical to me. Things are never really beautiful in themselves. They always need love to do them justice. The love of the beholder, I grant you that! But not only… In order to be really seen, to be appreciated to the full, they need to be seen together with him who made them. Only then they begin to shine, as they are recognized for what they really are: presents from his own hand. »

We were walking again. It was hot, and I was rather thirsty.

« I'll take an example from your churches, to help you see more clearly. »

« You know, I'm not that well informed concerning churches, » I said rather defiantly. « In fact, I'm not informed at all. And I don't miss it! »

The guide went on as if he hadn't heard me. « In your Christian churches you celebrate the Lord's supper. Now, what do you think the bread and the wine are standing for? »

« Heaven knows, » I said glumly, thinking of endless debates and scornful articles that had reached even my so uninterested ears.

« Well, think of it this way, » he continued, all the while brushing some particularly persistent flies from his forehead. « When you were small, your mother made you a birthday cake, right? So, when she put it before you, on your birthday, with a smile in her eyes, saying 'This is for you, lad!'… what did she put before you? »

« Er, a birthday cake? Sorry, I wasn't trying to be funny, but I don't see what you're getting at. »

« I tell you what she gave you then. Not just a lump containing a mixture of flour, eggs, milk… »

« Raisins, » I helped.

« Raisins, the whole mass sticking together by means of water and heat… »

« Doesn't sound very poetic, » I agreed.

« No, she put before you something into which she had poured her heart, all her love for you. This birthday cake was a little bit like love become solid. From Mum to Tim. Do you see? »

I did. But what about the churches…?

« If the churches are wise, they will understand this is true for the Lord's Supper, too. Let them argue about the ingredients, let them bore him, the center of it all, with suppositions, probabilities and certainties - as long as they see the Giver in the gift, things can't get too much out of hand. But if they don't see him any more, if bread and wine lose touch with him who says, 'From Me, to you, with all the Love I'm capable of !' - well, my son, then… »

« Then you've definitely got the wrong copy ! » I finished for him.

He shot me an appraising look. « You do get on, don't you?! Come, let's find some creek and make camp for the night. »

*****

9) SOUL SEARCHING

We passed by a very strange bush. Or was it something else? Hard to tell. Its colour was a mixture of soft green and a rather harsh yellow. It was full of silky buds, some of them already open. Weird tentacles were spreading out, moving, searching for something. It was lovely and ugly, familiar and totally alien at the same time.

« Let's sit down and observe it for a little while, » suggested the guide.

And so we did. As we were sitting there, lazily watching, nothing seemed to happen at first. But then, I heard a soft wail. I started.

« What was that? »

The guide pointed at the bushy thing. « Look, one of the buds is opening. »

While he was still talking, a slimy tentacle wriggled itself out, and a thin, rather squeaky little voice could be heard. At first I couldn't make out what it was saying, but after a while it got more familiar and I understood the words.

« Listen… listen… you have to listen to me… »

« What is all this about? » I asked, turning to my friend. But he just sat still, watching.

« You should … listen to me… always… always… always…. » said the voice with more resonance now. And then again, after a while, « You should … listen… »

« Thank you, yes, I got that far, » I grumbled. « But what should I listen to, you dumb creature? »

Immediately, as if it had heard my comment, the bush answered, « No matter … as long as you listen… obey me … obey my voice … my will … my desire… »

« Not a bit despotic, are you? » I scoffed.

My friend turned to me. « That's how you'd call it? Yes, I agree. »

« But what is it? » I asked, looking at the tentacles moving, whispering to themselves.

« It is called by different names in the world you come from. You'd call it 'soul', I guess. »

I was shocked upright. « A soul?! You must be kidding! A soul could never look like that … that weird thing over there! It's beautiful, the soul, or at least, it is supposed to be. They say it is God-given, he put something of himself into it. How dare you confound that creature over there with a soul! »

I started walking around agitatedly. My companion stayed where he was, looking at me with, surprisingly, approval in his eyes.

« Yes, » he said. « Yes, you're right. That's what the soul is like - originally. »

« Oh, stop it, with your Original and your fakes, » I said irritably.

« I told you I might harp on what I consider worth harping on, » he retorted mildly. « The soul is indeed a beautiful work of art, mirroring as it does the Maker himself. But, you see, this one went astray. It was uprooted, torn from its original ground, and it ended up here, and now it's turned all weird. Or despotic, as you said yourself. But if you look closely, you can still see its original beauty. »

I watched, silently. My heart was aching. « So - what happens to it now? »

« That depends. It cannot grow here, the soil's rotten. It has to be uprooted again, and replanted into the loamy soil where it came from. It won't agree easily, though. Uprooting hurts, and it's bound to lose a small part in the process. »

« You … should … listen… » the bush harped on, whispering fiercely now. « Listen … to me, to my desires … to my feelings … obey… »

I turned away, feeling very confused. « I don't understand. Since when is it wrong to listen to one's feelings and desires? I thought we'd finally got over all that stuff and found a bit of freedom at last. Don't tell me your Landowner wants us back to stuffy morals and rigid rules and heaps of 'thou shalt not's'… »

« Don't be ridiculous, » the guide said, rather curtly. « Of course he doesn't. These tentacles are not real desires. They're just bad cop… sorry, nearly did it again. » He smiled ruefully. « Real desires are a mirror of God himself. A strong will is a special gift from heaven. But - they have to stay just that, a mirror of God, a gift from heaven. The link with the Author has to be there, otherwise these qualities will turn sour. Look at this creature. Does its voice appeal to you? Does it look healthy? Does it look happy? »

« No, » I said. « No, you know it doesn't. It looks sick. It's just that … it's a bit shocking to see that something you believed in turns out to be so different from what you thought it to be… so out of place … it makes me feel sad. Sad, and a bit disgusted. Can we … do anything for it? Can we bring it back? »

« Not you, not now. But somebody's on his way already, the son I told you about. It's his job, he's the chief gardener. »

« And he'll just dig in his spade and bring it back to its original place? » I asked hopefully.

« No, » said my friend, and now he looked very serious. « No, in here you can't work like that. The laws of the place won't allow it. He can't just rip it out, but he will speak to it. He will ask if it is happy here. And if it is honest, it will say no, not really. And then he will ask for its permission to dig it out and bring it home, to be replanted in fertile soil. And it will be afraid and trembling and rustling. Or it will make a big show of itself and go all haughty and disdainful and ask the gardener not to meddle with things he doesn't understand anyway. Or it will fall silent and think. All this may take a long time. The gardener will lean on his spade and wait. »

« And then? » I asked in a tense voice.

« Then - well, it will either stay where it is and get more and more caught up in its own tentacles. Or it will consent - and the gardener will dig its roots up, very carefully, very lovingly, and bring it back to the place where it belongs. There it will recover, and return to its original splendour and health. Or it will wait, not daring to decide. In that case, the gardener will go away for a while, and come back later and try again.Try to talk it into reason. Try to evoke its original place, the lovely soil there, the colours it had and may have again…Oh, he'll try all right. He just loves these creatures, he does… Look, here he is! »

*****

10) RECOGNIZING

It was strange to see the waterfall again. This time it was an image, but it looked as real as the one I saw in the beginning. I wouldn't even have known it was only an image if it had not been shining through the man who came nearer, a spade on his shoulder, a greeting on his lips, the warmth in his eyes soothing the tension that automatically built up in me whenever more than one person was around.

The deep longing awoke again, and with it the surprising, but simple conviction that this man, this stranger, would just have to call me - and all the pieces would somehow come together, all would somehow be well.

« Call me, » I asked, hoarsely. « Call me to you. »

« Me » was listening, and trying to understand.

Me thought that, maybe, here was safety at last.

Me - who is me?

What a strange question. But what a true question…

« Come and meet my Father! » said the stranger.

The first thing I felt was fear.

Fear.

Not spiritually correct, I told myself, to feel fear in the presence of your very own Father. But then, there it was. Better face reality, even if you don't like it.

« Father, » I said, « I'm afraid. » I looked up, right into his eyes. I felt naked. Naked and extremely vulnerable.

« I know, » he said. Nothing else. No nice words of reassurance. Just that. He knew. But my heart sang.

What do you say to your Father when you're face to face and both of you have time?

I didn't know where to start. So I just sat there, quietly, in his presence. That seemed enough somehow.

But after a while a very old, very haunting question popped up in my head.

« Father, » I began, « what… »

« Wait, » he interrupted me. « Take your time. Just be here with me. Then, when you feel you're ready… »

So Me came forward.

I hadn't heard the call, but Me must have heard.

Me was feeling very sad, and small, and afraid. Me was weeping.

But then, knowing what it was to be known.

Me had a strange growth coming out of his head. I looked at it curiously and, after a while, with revulsion. It looked like a worm, creeping in and out of the head, slowly balancing from left to right, whispering then in this, then in that ear of Me. Softly hissing words I couldn't even begin to understand, but I saw Me could. Me nodded. Me looked hesitatingly at his Father and started backing away.

« No, don't listen to it! » I said sharply, and, turning to my Father, « Can't you see it is doing Me harm? Can't you stop it from talking? »

« I could, but the moment has not come yet. »

« The moment, the moment, » I parroted angrily. « If you don't stop the worm now, Me will become afraid of you and turn away again. Look, it's happening already! »

And yes - Me, with an anxious look, turned and went away, slowly, haltingly, looking more vulnerable than ever.

I would have run after the lonely figure, but my Father held me back. « Don't upset him. I could tear the worm out, but it is still too much entwined with him. I just can't take the risk of tearing parts of him away. Be patient. I'll not leave him. We'll not leave him. We'll go and talk to him and, if he decides to listen, he will take hold of the worm himself. He will hold it at its roots, and present it to me, and ask me to heal him. And I will. The worm will not have the last word. Not over my dead body! »

« Seems to me you were quicker in Bible times, » I said, still smouldering.

He smiled. « There were times - and there still are, mind you! - when I command time to bypass itself, so to speak, when I feel it necessary. But even when my heart tells me to, I won't always do so. I didn't for my own son... »

He paused for a while, deep in thought. « How I would have loved just tearing time apart, tearing the world apart, tearing evil apart, » he said, as to himself. « That would have taught them! But no, it wouldn't, I knew it wouldn't. So I gritted my teeth. I took time, I took evil, I took humanity, I took reality, I took my son and I took myself, and I moulded it all into something totally new. It was hard - you cannot even begin to imagine how hard it was, but it was worth it. »

He looked at me. And he repeated : « Yes, it was worth it. »

Then he nodded to the guide. « Come, let's follow the Me. »

*****

11) SHADOWING

Suddenly I saw it. My heart made a queer jump, and I felt a rush of anger surging through me. « Go away! », I snarled, and again, « Get going - now! »

The whatever it was had stopped at my first shout. It stood there, quietly, looking utterly lost for a moment. Then it slinked away into the forest. I felt my guide looking at me, but he didn't say anything.

« I somehow thought it wouldn't follow me here, » I thought it necessary to explain. « It's awful, I can't seem to get rid of it. »

Still my companion remained silent. I was on the defensive. « Why should I let it come near me? » I asked, rather savagely. « It spoils everything, it always does. As soon as I see it, things start going wrong. I feel tired.

I feel sad for no apparent reason, it's as if a big bleak shadow creeps up and follows me around wherever I go. So, at least I try to keep it at a distance. »

« What would happen if you'd let him come near? » inquired my friend.

« Heaven knows, » I snapped. « It's bad enough when it stays away. »

« Do you think he would come any nearer if you asked him? »

I stared at him. « Sorry, but I don't understand. Why should I? »

He bit his lip. « Well, if he follows you around, there may be a reason. Why not just ask him? »

I knew him enough by now to understand that he wouldn't say a thing like that without having a very clear idea indeed why he said it - so I answered, « You can as well tell me what you think about him - about it, I mean. »

« Him, » he corrected easily. « Yes, I can tell. But I'd rather he told you himself. Here he is again. Will you trust me, and ask him to come a bit nearer? »

My heart started beating faster again when I felt, more than I saw, the familiar shadow appear at the edge of the forest, waiting shyly.

I wanted to say something, but no words came out. I tried again. « Would… would you come, ah, nearer, if you please? » I told myself angrily that I sounded like a timid boy asking an equally timid girl for a dance, but the shadow understood all right and eagerly started forward.

« Stop! » I shouted harshly.

It stopped dead in its tracks. I felt my guide squeezing my shoulder. « Go on, don't be afraid, I'm with you, » he whispered.

« Sorry, I mean, sorry… » I continued lamely. « I … actually, I do want you to come nearer, it's just… well, okay, if you have to know, it's just that I'm afraid of you. There. Afraid. Do you hear? »

The creature had heard, apparently. It nodded its tiny head. This was rather ugly, like all the rest, by the way. But now there was the ghost of a smile on its lips. Not a sneer, I noticed. A nice smile, a shy one, but a smile nevertheless.

« You can come, if you wish, » I heard myself say. Well, yes, why not? My heart was already hammering away like a sputtering, broken down engine. I already felt like I was being sucked up by a monstrous giant hoover, so it couldn't get any worse.

The shadow tiptoed some yards nearer. I moaned. Had I said it couldn't get any worse?

« I'm not a monster. »

The voice was light, a bit high, rather like a child's. It gave me a start. Where had I heard it before? And what did it say? I'm not a monster? No, maybe not, but I felt so terribly afraid. So I told him, « I know you aren't. I can see that now. I'm sorry. But I fear you nevertheless. Why do you always follow me ? Why do you come back, again and again? »

He shrugged his shoulders. « Where do you want me to go? I need a place to stay, and I belong to you. Where else can I go? »

I felt strangely touched. I belong to you, he had said. Belong? To me?

« I'm part of you, » he volunteered further information. « I am all that you hate because I am all that you hid. »

I stayed silent. So did my friend.

« I'm your not nice-ness, your not-correctness… I'm your anger, your pain, your anguish…name it, you don't want it, I am it. »

I stared at the child, for now I saw that that was what the shadow had hidden. Strange, deep, wild emotions surged through me.

« I'm a little bit dead, but not completely, » continued the child. « I'm not dead, oh no, I cannot die, but I cannot live either - not this way. That's why I have to follow you as a shadow. Please, won't you allow me to live? »

I looked at my guide, helplessly. « It's strange, I don't want him to live, and at the same time I do. But... how can I help him? »

The answer was simple. « Let's call him. »

« Call him? Even nearer?! »

« No, not just even nearer. Right into you. Together we'll call him. He will recognize our voices, and he will come back to life. The pieces will come together, and they will become a part of you again, but this time they will be united, and they will have their place, and you will become whole again. But you have to give the child his place. His place, mind you - not all the place! Nor the small stow-away cave he had to hide in before. A real place. His own. Let's call. »

And that's what we did.

It took some time, though.

*****

12) LOOKING FOR THE LOST ONES

There was a noise coming from the direction we were going. It floated up to us as on the wings of the wind. I heard voices, children's voices I thought, and a woman singing. When we were near enough to see and hear more clearly, my guide took me by the hand, put his finger on his lips and whispered, « Let's not disturb them. We'll sit down here and just watch them for a while.

The children didn't seem very happy. They were all sitting quite far away from each other, every one eyeing his neighbour with mistrust and defiance. The woman was going from one to the other, talking to them.

They watched her warily, too, but at least they seemed to listen to her.

She was just coming up to the little boy sitting nearest to us, and I got a real shock when he turned his back to her and so happened to look straight into my face. There was such a harshness there… No child had the right to look like that. His eyes were cold and rejecting, it was as if they had frozen in the middle of his face.

I looked questioningly at my friend. His face was sad as he returned my look. « Yes, » he whispered softly. « I know. It's weird, but then, you don't know his story. This is how he became. Listen to what the woman is going to say. »

The woman had stopped at a little distance from the child, who looked at her askance. She went on her knees. « Can I sit here for a little while? » she asked respectfully. The child hesitated for a second, then nodded. The woman took her time, chose a flat place in the grass near the child, and sat down quietly, looking at the ground.

Seeing that she didn't come any nearer nor threaten him in any way, and was seemingly content just to sit there, the child visibly relaxed and didn't turn from her any more.

After a while he even began to look expectantly at his new companion, as if waiting for something to happen. And then the woman began to sing, very softly, nearly murmuring, but there was a definite melody to it, a hauntingly sad but beautiful tune that went right into my heart.

This is what she sang:

Bitter one, little one,
How did you get like this?
What did you see, what did you hear,
How has it hurt your heart?
How bravely did you fight, my child,
You tried, you fell, got up again,
But in the end you just gave up,
You were so very tired...
There was no help in sight, was there?
So then you turned against yourself.

You said, 'I'll be in charge of me.
You taught me that I'm all alone?
Well then, alone I'll be.
I'll go for bitterness myself,
Because my own is sweet,
Compared to the inflicted one,
The one I can't escape,
The one that struck me down.

So now I choose my bitterness,
My own, my own, my very own,
And I will never leave it.'

Come, little one,
This is no good…
Look, can you see my flowers?
Come, touch and smell, and feel that here's
No hurt, no dirt, no rudeness…
They are for you,
They're all for you,
Come, smell the Father's goodness…

The boy sat there, rigidly, as if he hadn't heard a word.

But when the woman stretched out a hand, tentatively, he took it and allowed himself to be led towards the center of the field where two other children were already sitting. He sat down, a bit grudgingly, but clearly in sight of the other two, who greeted him silently, with just a slight nod of their heads.

I was weeping. I couldn't help it.

« Will the harshness be gone from his face? » I asked the guide.

He nodded. « Yes, it will, but it will take time… a lot of time, and a lot of singing. Would you like to stay here and see how she talks to the other children, or would you rather go on? »

« No, let's stay here, » I answered. « I want to hear more. »

The woman had stayed a while with the three children, but now she was walking to another boy at the far end of the field. I hadn't even seen him at first, he must have dug himself a hole in the ground for I could just see the top of a head sticking out. The head quickly disappeared when the child saw the woman approaching, but when she stopped and waited it popped out again, dodging in and out of its hole like a frightened rabbit. I found that, even at that distance, I could see and hear quite well.

The woman stayed where she was, addressing her song to the child:

> Hating one, little one,
> Far back your story goes…
> They slapped and struck and hunted you,
> Until you found this place.
> It hid you well, it was your home,

A hole, deep in the ground.
Hating one, little one,
I ask you, no, I beg you,
Come out of there, just once, my child,
And meet my smile, it's real.
I know you, child, I truly do.
You didn't want to be
So hard and dark, so tight and tense...
This is no place for you.
Please, come with me, come home with
    me,
The stove is on, it's nice and warm,
And if you're not at ease,
You go back here, sleep in your hole,
But come at least and visit me,
I'm longing to receive you...
And in the end all will be well
For I will never leave you.

On and on the woman went, on and on she
sang:

Angry one, little one,
How angry are your eyes!
How fiercely do you look at me!
I understand it well.
I want to give

What you don't want,
I want to comfort you…
You frown, 'Not sad! I'm angry, me!'
But sadness calls for anger…
I do know why, for I have seen,
And I have come to hold you,
To hold you close, against my heart,
It's beating with your anger.
For I am angry too, with those
Who hurt my child so badly -
So we are two! And that takes out
The poison the most deadly.

Cynical one, little one,
You had no right to be…
They said you were not nice, my child,
Not good, not good enough…
So many times you had to hide,
You couldn't be yourself;
So many times you were shut out,
But did they tell you why?
You had prepared so large a space
For people in your heart…
For beauty, goodness, life and joy,
The treasures life can hold…
And when they did not come, your heart

Closed up, dried out, fell silent…
No loving water flowing there,
And only desert left…
And in that desert, little one,
You built yourself a throne,
And on that throne you sit and smirk,
'I see you from above!
Let no one come and bully me
- do this, do that, this way, no, that -
For now it's me who reigns!
And I will trust no more, you hear?
No person and no word.
I'll listen only to my voice,
The tune of inner sadness,
The tune of hardness and of pride,
For that at least sounds true…
And all that has some nice sweet taste,
I will condemn as fake;
Yes, this will be my sure defense,
The strongest walls on earth…
No one will ever guess or see
The many scars I bear,
So strong it is, so sure it is,
My prison of despair…'

Cynical one, little one,
Your tower is so high…
So hard a climb, so long a climb,
But I will come, I promise.
And maybe you will even come
And join me there, halfway?
So that, at last, our hands can touch
And our eyes can meet…
For you are not afraid of me?
Child, I could never hurt you.
I only want to heal, to help,
I want to do you good.
And I would like to sing for you,
A song, for you alone.
I only ask you, listen now,
That is enough for me.
For once I've sung you can go back,
High up into your tower;
My song - it will have struck a chord,
Because by Love it's driven…
It'll wake a tune, of something lost,
Of something found - that's given.

Sad one, little one,
You do not understand.
You don't need to!

Come here, to me,
Be welcome in my heart.
I don't know what to say, my child,
I cannot find the words,
The words you need, but I have arms,
And these, these are wide open!
I hope so much that you will come,
I'd be so glad - I'm waiting…
What? I should come? Should come
    myself ?

…………

Well, here I am, and gladly!
There's just one thing;
I am myself,
And not your expectation…
I give, but not all that you wish
For I am who I am…
But what I have, I truly give,
Which means, the very best!
And you will see, it is enough,
Your heart will be at rest.

Blind one, little one,
You fear you have to see,
In order to be loved?!

Little blind one, just come with me,
We'll go and find the Father,
We'll go and ask together, child,
If he, at last, will heal you.
But since at present you're still blind,
I'll take your hand and lead you.

Dead one, little one,
Poor one, know,
You are not dead. Not dead!
I see you move,
I see your eyes,
You try to lift your head!
I know how bad it was, my child,
But be assured, it's over.
Yes, I have seen, and yes, I know,
What you would like to say,
'Where were you, then? There was no
    help…
Why did you let it happen?'
I do not answer, child, not yet,
But know that I was hurt
As much as you - and deeper still,
My own bones have been aching.
And now you laugh, my child - I'm glad! -
'A God, he has no bones!'

Believe me, child, I once had bones,
I know how they can hurt...
Come now to me - ah, there you are!
I'll hold you close, forever.
Come eat with me, come rest with me,
And slowly you'll recover.

Happy child, little child,
Hidden, loved and joyful child,
I am so glad that you are there,
For you can help the others.
You never lost the Kingdom's taste,
You never lost its sight,
You went on singing, dancing, child,
You knew there was real life.
So I do ask you, come and take
The others by the hand,
You are the one who understands,
And they hear what you say;
You're one of them, they'll follow you,
And you can show the way.

Angry child, little child,
Hating child, cynical child,

Bitter child, sad child,
Blind child, dead child…-
Look, it is not too late!
For here's your Father calling you,
Each one by his own name!
Yes, here he is, to bring you home,
The Author of my song!
And so, together, all in one
You'll be, and you'll belong.

I wept. I didn't mind. The tears were welling up all of their own, and I let them flow freely.

The guide didn't do or say anything, but I felt he understood. I knew he did, and I knew he understood more deeply than I could ever understand myself, and I was comforted.

Through a haze I saw the woman approaching, leading the children by their hands. They came to a halt before us, and she addressed an inquiring look at my friend.

« Is he ready? » she asked.

« I think so, » he answered.

Then, with a smile, she turned to me and, with a last encouraging look at the children, put the little hand of one of them into mine, prodded the others forward, and left.

The guide nodded. « Take them. They're yours. »

*****

13) FLEEING OR FACING

Footsteps came nearer - running footsteps. Breathing hard, a man came round the corner of the path. As he passed by, he shot us only a furtive look, for his attention was completely concentrated on something apparently behind him, following him hard on his heels. And yes, a short time afterwards we heard another noise… soft, padding footsteps, now, but running, running, too.

As the grey shadow appeared, my heart gave a jump, and my legs turned watery. I nearly started running myself, but my friend took me by the arm and held it in a surprisingly strong grip. « Don't, » he warned, « don't, or it might turn round and follow you. »

It was a difficult moment, especially as the shadow, coming nearer, slowed its pace and looked at me out of queer yellow eyes. I shuddered, but stood firm, feeling my friend's supporting and comforting hold.

The shadow sniffed at me, shook itself and then left us, loping behind the man, accelerating its pace. We stood silent.

Then I heard it, the scream I was expecting. It cut through me, for it could have been mine, and had been before.

I heaved a deep sigh, but I felt better, now that the thing had gone. My friend let go of my arm. « Did you recognize it? » he asked.

I nodded. « I've felt it before. Often. It's horrible, isn't it? … But then, you and your Landlord wouldn't know, » I added, a little bitterly.

He gave me a strange look. « How would you know? We live here, and the shadow is extremely powerful. Don't you think it could follow us, too? »

« But you seemed to know how to handle it, » I protested. « You told me to stand, and not to run. »

« Exactly, » he nodded. « But that's because we know it so well. My friend, the Landlord's son, learned how to approach it. He learned not to run, even if his legs told him they'd run first and ask for permission later. He learned to look right into its face. »

« And that makes it go away? »

He shook his head. « No. At least, most of the time it doesn't. But, strangely enough, learning to stand in its presence is the best way to defend yourself. For as soon as you run, it will run after you, and most of the time it will outrun you.

« And then? » I asked, thinking of the scream.

« It will attack you, and grip you, and hold you in its claws. Sometimes it will overcome you and strike you down. But most often it will be just happy to hold you and prevent you from going on - what's more, prevent you from doing or even thinking anything at all. »

Suddenly I felt angry. « Well, the master of this land really seems to make a mess of it, doesn't he?, » I blurted out. « Not even able to prevent monsters like this one from roaming freely around the place. Don't tell me there are more of them. »

« As many as there are people here, » he answered.

« So why doesn't he get the forest cleared up, once and for all? Or doesn't he care? Well, it's not his problem after all, sitting high and dry in some protected place… »

My friend turned round and looked me fully in the eyes. « He himself succumbed while facing it, » he said. « He came out of the fight so full of wounds… if I hadn't known him so closely, I'd hardly have recognized him myself. The scars are there even now. »

I didn't answer, moodily walking on. Too many questions, too few answers.

The guide went on, more cheerful now. « Come, don't be discouraged. True, the shadow will come after you, too, again and again. But it will not overcome you, not with me around. You know, when the master fought it, he gave it a mortal blow, and it lost its almighty strength.

So you can stand, and look it in the face. Only don't think you can escape it, or jump over it, or avoid it altogether. Some people think that they can make it go away, the master of the place being who he is, but he himself couldn't escape, and his name bears witness to that. »

« His name? » Suddenly I remembered the man I'd met, the deep impression he'd made on me, the sheer power of his reality. Strange - imagine that someone like him could succumb to anything, let alone to a shadow-creature of his own land... « What did you say his name was? »

« He has many names. But one of them is: He-who-bears-the-shadow. »

« That doesn't help much... does the shadow itself have no name, then? »

« But of course, » said my friend. « It is called 'pain'. »

I was not satisfied, and he knew it. He smiled. « Ask ahead! »

I tried to put some order into the questions in my head, but they seemed to run around as fast as the shadow itself.

« Just start anywhere, » he said encouragingly.

Hesitatingly, thinking of my own experience, I did. « When the shadow grips you, why does it not only hurt you so to speak on the outside, but also right inside? Why does it get its claws on the heart itself, and why does it feel as if he's tearing it out of you, leaving you all naked and open and empty? »

He thought for a while, then said, « It's the character of the thing - I can't tell you much more. It's the way it attacks, but you are right... if it would just hurt people on the outside they would not be so terribly afraid of it. »

« And what did you mean when you said it could not overcome me, not with you around? I don't understand. You told me afterwards that it would not necessarily get any less ferocious, even with someone like you for company, and, well, apparently it didn't with the boss of this place, anyway... »

He nodded. « True. But if you know I'm with you, it will nevertheless change the impact of the attack. How can I explain it? You will see the shadow itself differently, as if its colour had changed... »

I thought back. « It was grey, wasn't it? At least I think it was. »

« For you it was. It's a bit like a cameleon. Sometimes it will appear a flaming red; then it will turn a dull lilac, or a dirty brown, or a deep black; or it will look a chilling grey, as you saw it just now. It all depends on the poison. In fact, it is not the shadow itself that is the most dangerous, it's the poison it carries. If it were just a shadow, it would be more bearable. It would bite, and leave a hurting wound, and go away. But it's the poisons that go with it; they burn their way down into the heart, if you let them, and will eat it from the inside. There are very nasty ones. »

He saw my look. « I'll give you an example. There's the one called 'I did something wrong'. As it starts to flow through your veins, you start to repeat it to yourself, 'I did something wrong, wrong, wrong,' until your whole body is echoing with it. Then it subtly changes colour, as it becomes 'I *am* wrong, I'm all wrong, all in me is wrong.' That's when it eats you from the inside. »

I shuddered. Too well I knew what he was talking about.

« Why did you say, 'if you let them'? » I whispered. « Is there anything you can do then, to stop the poisons from eating into the heart? »

He looked at me gravely. « Yes, there is. You can recognize the danger, and be warned. And then, when the shadow comes upon you and bites, you can tell it, 'I can't stop you biting me, but I refuse your poison.' »

« And that's enough? » I asked doubtfully.

« Yes. But you should say it again and again. Also, it will help a lot to set your mind on me, on my face, my words. Remember that I'm always with you, always on your side, whether you see me, hear me or feel me - or not. That's very important. For the poison blurs your eyesight, and so I might suddenly seem to be your enemy, as if I were with the shadow, together with it, against you. Remember, the poison has that effect. So hold on to what I have told you, and what is the truth: I am on your side, so there's the two of us facing them, the shadow and its lies, and we'll go for them together. »

« I have a last question. You told me not to run away from the shadow. But surely we should try to avoid it, if possible? You wouldn't want me to go looking for it, would you? »

« Of course not », he said, rather vehemently. « How foolish that would be! Never go looking for it, and by all means try to avoid it, if that is possible without losing your way and your purpose. But you see, that man running away from it, the one you just saw before, was determined to do anything - anything at all, in order to escape it. He left his path, he pushed others out of the way, he made them fall, trodding over them, and if necessary he would even have killed them if they'd prevented him from escaping. He completely lost his direction, he didn't know any more where he was going, just that he was going away from something. And that is the shadow's real power and threat. Not the biting, sometimes not even the poison that comes with it, but to make people so afraid that, trying to escape it whatever the cost, they are completely in its grip. »

*****

14) TURNING ROUND
AND ROUND

What a strange sight it was… we had come upon a round wall, made of some sort of glass, I thought, because I could see right through it. Behind the wall a bunch of people were trodding in a circle, each person following the one before him, marching mechanically… When I looked at one of them, a man, I saw an empty, glazed look on his face. It was as if some unseen puppeteer was drawing him forward, making his legs move, his hands dangle and his head nod slightly up and down. It gave me a queer feeling in my stomach.

The guide looked at them, too, a sad smile on his lips.

« We call it different names, » he said. « Illusion's circle - or the misery-go-round of abuse - or the prison of things. So easy to get in - so hard to get out... »

« But why would people ever want to get in? » I asked, bewildered. « Don't they see how ugly it all is? »

« No, that's the problem, they don't. The thing is, when somebody enters the circle, tentatively maybe at first, it gives him or her a certain pain, but also a certain pleasure. In a way, it is a gratifying experience. So they say, 'let's try another step, see how it goes.' And it gives them a queer kind of satisfaction. Another step follows, and another, and before they know it, they're right in the circling movement, and they don't know how to get out - or how they got into it in the first place... The movement holds them captive, they become its slave. So sad... »

After a while he went on, pensively. « You see that one, for instance. » He pointed to a man with a pale face, sluggishly plodding forward. « He only got in two weeks ago. He is in the victim-place right now. He's telling himself the same thing over and over again:

'People hurt me. Every one hurt me. So they owe me a debt. Every one owes me, the world owes me, God owes me a debt, for I've suffered, and I've suffered too much. There's a big hole in me now, made by all the things I've never had, and it has the right to be filled. By my wife. By my children. By my friends. By my neighbours. By God. They shall fill it. They must. They have to. They owe me this.'

See, and now he gets on to the next place. It's called frustration. Here he says:

'They don't pay the debt. They don't live up to my rightful expectations. I hate them.'

Now he is in the persecutor's place, saying:

'So it's my turn to hurt *them*.'

Then he takes another step, and now he finds himself in the area of the guilt-feelings. Very strange, that one, it's flexible, it can pop up at any time and at any place of the circle. It moves with the people, so to speak. Here he says to himself:

'Nasty one, who are you to hate the people this way? You know very well you should not. See how worthless you are - you don't even try to be more Christian. God's angry with you. Hurry up, repent and repair. Otherwise darkness will be your lot. If it isn't already.' »

I shuddered. « And he really says that to himself? »

The guide looked at me seriously. « Not at first, no », he admitted. « But it's what other people told him, and slowly he started to believe them, and then to repeat those words to himself. »

« I remember. That was what the woman said to one of the children. But why do people say those things in the first place? »

« Because in fact it's not just the guilt-feelings that accompany the people, it's the invisible enemy himself. He uses them as a tool in his hand - and what a disastrous tool it is. »

I stared at my friend, a bit frightened. « The invisible enemy? I remember you mentioned him before. Who is he, then? And where is he? - Well no, if he's invisible, I won't be able to recognize him, would I? But who is he? And where does he come from? »

My guide turned to look at the people. He went on as if he hadn't heard my questions. « At the next step he says:

'Every one's angry with me anyway. I hate them. No, I don't. Yes, I do. No, I should not. Yes, I should. It's all their fault. It's all my fault.'

And then he goes on to the next place, which is also called the victim-place, but it is a variation. Do you see that the landscape here is slightly different from the first one ? But in the end - or should I say in the beginning? - it leads to the same conclusion. Here he says:

'So what ? So I'm alone. I am ALONE. I will have to take care of me and all and everything MYSELF. There's nobody to care for me and to take care of me, there has never been and there never will be. So I'll have to do the filling myself. I'll fill what others left open, I'll take what others didn't give, I'll force them to pay the debt they owe. And as they didn't care what they did to me, so I won't care what I'll do to them, and I'll have my revenge.' »

« That's horrible, » I sighed.

« Isn't it? But he suffers the same pain he's inflicting on others now. He thinks he's taking sweet revenge, but he's only getting more and more imprisoned in his circle. He'll never be able to satisfy himself this way, to make up for his wants, to fill the holes within - for they cannot be filled by what I call things. »

« Things? »

« Yes. Things are like frames robbed of their pictures, envelopes without their letters, admiration without respect, lust without love, the appearance of life without life itself. They are dark and interesting things, with dark and interesting owners… They're like drugs, they satisfy your thirst for a moment, until you need a second shot. The more you fill yourself with things, the more you need them, and the more you will go out of your way - litterally too - to get them… and get lost. »

« Then they're condemned to stay in the circle, once they're in? It seems so cruel, so unfair a prison… »

« It is, » admitted my friend, « but it's part of the package called reality-and-its-laws, and that one, in its turn, is part of another, called freedom of choice. »

« I don't like these packages, » I said emphatically.

« Let's say, the result is not very nice, no. The Original was planned differently, of course. But there you are… you cannot give the present called freedom and then take it back as soon as you see how badly it is used. It's in the character of the present that it can be used in a wonderful or in a bad way; so either you give it or you don't. - As to your question, if they're condemned to stay in the circle, no, they aren't. Definitely not! You'll see afterwards. »

« I still don't understand this filling-thing, » I said. « You told me before that those people tried to fill themselves with things that will never satisfy them. But what do you mean? And is there something else that would do the job? »

« Of course! » he laughed. « The Original always does! As before, we're talking about bad copies here, or, to use a different example, about pictures torn from their frames. Do you see that man over there, walking past the bushes, with the spectacles and the grey hair? He wants attention. He's craving for it, mad for it. And it is true that, as a child, he did not have it. Not enough. He has too many atten-tion-holes in him, so to speak. So now he tries to fill them with attention-things, by which I mean, any attention, anyhow, by anyone, at any moment. Robbed of its context.

You see, normally attention is a result. A fruit of a real relationship, a real dialogue. It is worthwhile only as a whole, when it is freely given.

But this man is so desperately looking for it that he will steal to possess it, taking it out of the frame of relationship and personality to make it his own. In doing this, he humili-ates the other person, considering him only as a means by which attention can be obtained. That person becomes a mere thing, an object, useful because it provides the necessary filling for gaping attention-holes…

But as a thing will never fill a human being, that man over there will need seas and seas of attention, he will drink and drink and never be satisfied. »

« I see, » I murmured. And indeed I did. And I saw something else, too.

My friend looked at me. « You can talk about it, you know, » he said, very gently. « You don't have to, of course. But you can. Choose your moment, take your time. »

« It… it is… do you think that can also happen with… other things? » I blurted out. « I mean… let's say, with the body, too? »

« Yes, » he answered quietly. « Yes, it can happen with the body, too. Somebody with holes in him, or her, will take the body of someone else, he will tear that beautiful picture out of its frame, and rip it apart; then he will take the pieces to fill in the holes. He claims the other's body as his own to possess it, and thereby reduces it, and the person, to a thing. But at the same time he reduces it to something which will never ever really give him what he needs, so he hurts himself as well as the other… He stays thirsty, and then convinces himself he needs more and other things, and if only he could lay his hands on them, everything would be all right. And round and round he goes… and the enemy laughs his head off…

The horrible thing is that this man doesn't even care about the picture itself, he just cuts it into pieces that will fit into the holes… »

« But, » I stammered, « does that mean that the… the picture is destroyed, then? That it cannot be restored? »

« No, » said the guide in a very sure voice. « No, the picture cannot be destroyed, the laws of the Maker forbid it. But it can be severely damaged, and it will take a lot of time to restore it, and the hand of the greatest expert. »

My head felt as if it would burst, so I hastily changed the subject. « What about the something that can fill the holes? »

He smiled. « As I said, it's the Original. For instance, whereas the bad copy is the attention-thing, the Original is a true relationship. Or communion. It is a beautiful gift, and it has a great capacity of healing and restoring. I will tell you more about it in a moment, but let's have something to eat first, shall we? »

After we had eaten he continued. « One of the next steps this man will take is the one of the abuse itself, or, if you prefer, the illusion of filling. Then my guess is that either he'll justify himself, saying that the other has not suffered any more than he has, or he'll go on into another guilt-phase. He will look at himself in horror, and despise himself. He then enters into condemnation, but comes out of it telling himself it's too late to change, and he wouldn't know how to anyway, because his holes start to hurt even more. They have only been filled in an illusionary way, and so they will shout louder, like young birds crying for food, and the man will become bolder and more tyrannic, and want more of the same thing here and now. »

I wanted to ask if there was no hope left then, when I saw strange shadows flitting in and out of the circle.They approached the people and seemed to push them on, from one place to another, on and on.

« What are those? » I asked curiously.

« They are called helpers, » the guide explained.

« Helpers?! They don't seem to help a great deal, » I snorted. « They just make the others go round a bit faster. »

He nodded. « It's rather complicated. Those shadows are either the thoughts of the shuffling ones themselves, or those of other people coming into their field. They think they help them, but, as you so very rightly said, they only urge them on. Listen to the one who is talking to the man going through the victim-place now. »

Straining my ears, I could hear the words:

'Oh, my poor one, how horrible everything is, how awful. And how unlucky you are, and how bad it all is.'

« Yes, that is a real help », I sniffed.

« Isn't it?! And now further over there, in the abuser-field… »

A woman's voice was saying:

'Oh, how awful. People should not see this, imagine the shame on the family. I'll make it invisible because I love you, no one will ever know…'

« Talking about love, » I said indignantly. « Helping him to stay in the circle more than getting out of it! »

« So it is, » nodded my guide.

« But what will really help him? Help him to get out, I mean? And where can he get out? Isn't there a sort of special place, where the magic of the circle is less strong, where he has a chance to escape? »

« There is. The walls. »

« The walls?! But it's them that shut the people in most effectively! »

« At any place in the circle the people can get out. But they have to break through or jump over the walls. What do you think they are made of? »

« I don't know, they are transparent, but I don't know how solid they are. Looks like some sort of glass to me. »

« They're made of mirrors, but not ordinary ones. They are lying mirrors. They reflect the images of the people, but in a distorted way. They too are tools in the hand of the enemy. The mirrors laugh and point and say:

'Look at you, look who you are, what a flop, what a failure! Why would anybody care for you? See what you do, see who you are! We, we show you who you are, how disgusted we are... What? Try to get out?! - Come and try, try, make a run, head for us and see yourself, hurt yourself. We'll hurtle you back to where you are... try again, oh, how stupid one can be...' »

My throat was dry. « So? »
« So it needs him, » said my friend.

In contrast to the shuffling figures the man who was entering the circle now looked terribly real and solid. The waterfall shone from his face as clearly as when I had seen him for the first time. He walked with the people, sometimes talking to them, arguing with them, sometimes just accompanying them silently, going with them from one stage to another, supporting them when they stumbled. But always, at regular intervals, he would invite them to look at him, not dumbly at the ground or wildly at the mirrors, but at him.

And I saw that, once a figure managed to look up at him, something strange happened.

A smile seemed to flick through the air; like a spark it flew from the stranger's eye to the looking man or woman, and as it grew brighter and brighter, the walls seemed to shrink. And then the miracle happened. The figure stopped shuffling. It always did. What happened afterwards was different from one figure to another, but all of them stopped.

Some just seemed to gather strength on the spot, and, taking the hand of the stranger, they broke through the shuddering wall.

Others needed more time.

Still others fell into their walk again, but even in them something had changed, their eyes were more alert now, not just fixed on the ground, or flicking from one mirror to another. They watched the stranger until, by and by, they too had gathered enough strength from him - and then, together, they leapt over the wall.

And some, after a moment, started shuffling again, as if the words of the stranger were too beautiful to be true - or they themselves too weary to listen.

But then I saw more people coming into the field; solid they were, like the stranger, even if they didn't have his unique realness. They started to go with the remaining figures, helping them, supporting them, comforting and strengthening them, urging them to break out, taking them by the hand and leaping; in short, faithfully following the stranger's example. From time to time they waved to him, and he smiled at them, calling out words I could not understand.

« So they can escape, » I said slowly. « There is a way out. »

« There always is, » said my friend. « Because of him, there always is. »

****

15) FALLING IN LOVE

It was a lovely smell. It reminded me of those bright lavender fields in the Provence, the sun-warmed paths surrounded by thyme… Yes, it was like a smell, but also like a colour, or a rainbow of colours, dancing before the eyes… And then, it was also like music, or like birds singing in the early morning, when the dewdrops glisten in the first rays of the sun, changing from red to blue and green as you move… It was all of this, but still more - much more.

« I like your description, » my friend said. « It's all of that - and much more. It's called love. »

I suddenly grew cold, all cold inside. A helpless feeling overtook me, not vehemently, rather gently even. It was familiar, and I gave in to it. Without knowing why, I turned my head aside and let myself float into nothingness.

« Where are you going? »

I didn't react, why should I? I found myself gliding further and further away, into a sort of comfortable emptiness that would be terrible if it weren't for its familiarity, like a butterfly finding its way back into the cocoon, and settling down there...

« Come back! » The voice to my right rang with authority, and with something else, too. I heard it, but it didn't fit in the cocoon, it was all unreal, it was... yes, alive. Disturbing. Why being alive? When you can sleep... Being alive is being alone; much too threatening, to tell you the truth...

« That's not the truth ! Come to me - *I* am the truth! »

And with these words, it was as if a cloud lifted, a thick grey cloud, and I found that I could breathe again, and what was more, see.

I looked at the face of my friend, and my heart did a summersault, for it was just shining with… yes, with that beautiful smell and colour and music and light we so unceremoniously call love. I sighed.

« I'm so glad you came back, » he said simply.

« Well - you told me to, didn't you? »

He smiled. « Yes, but you came! »

« Where was I anyway? » I still felt dizzy.

« In your story. In a part of your reality, which is not a bad thing in itself. Only you mistook it for The Reality, or for The Truth, if you like. Alone, for ever and ever, Amen. Wasn't it like that? »

« Yes. Yes, that was how it felt. Strange, for it was horrible, but at the same time it was, well, so *familiar*, and I wanted it. I wanted to go there, even if I didn't…That doesn't make sense, does it? I'm sorry, I can't explain… »

« You don't need to, » he said, very gently. « I know. »

« Do you? » I hadn't wanted to sound so sceptical.

« Oh yes, remember, it's part of my friend's story, too. But that's where the Truth was born: you, Tim, can't be alone any more. You can feel alone, but you aren't. In the center of your life there is light. In the center of your life all is well. »

« It certainly didn't feel like that, » I said rebelliously.

« No, maybe not. Real presence doesn't depend on feelings; they will come and go. They are not reliable, because someday, somewhere, they got hurt. So they are like crazy signposts; one moment they'll tell you the right direction, and the next they'll mislead you completely. Don't take your feelings for a guide. »

« So what can I trust then ? »

The answer was as straight as it was simple. « Me! »

It was some hours later, and we were sitting in the evening sun.

« Why did it happen? » I asked. « This utter loneliness and emptiness, how did it get hold of me? »

My friend stayed silent for a while, watching the bright orange ball sinking slowly behind the dark line of fir trees on the far side of a field full of blooming heather.

« Because you were in touch with love. »

« Well, that's nice, » I said bitterly. « Thanks for the experience, but I'd rather not go through it again. »

« Many - most things are far from perfect - yet perfectly beautiful. »

*****

16) SEEING

« Can you give me an example? Of something imperfect but beautiful? »

He laughed. « By all means! Take love! You can be in touch with it, every day of your life. Whenever you meet people. »

« That's not love! » I protested vehemently.

« You see? There you go again. True, my friend, it doesn't come up to your impossible standards of what-it-should-be. But take them off, those dark glasses of yours, and what do you see? Tiny bits of real love. - No, I don't ask you to become naïve - », he said hastily, seeing the expression on my face. « But I do ask you to see *better*, more clearly. Wait, I'll show you what I mean. I'll lend you *my* glasses for a moment. »

For a little while I didn't see anything clearly. Images whirled through my head, chasing each other as in a mad game. Images of my mother, my father, of friends, of people from my office.

Then things seemed to settle, and I began to see.

I saw my mother, holding out her arms to me.

I saw myself, repeating obstinately, 'It's not real anyway, it's not real anyway…'

And it was true, there was a part of self-centeredness, a part where she needed me, a part that wanted me to be and to behave in a way that she thought correct.

But - and this came as a shock to me - that was *not* all! Under these layers I had so sovereignly classified as « not authentic » there was something deeper, something real and beautiful. A sob went through me. Something real, something beautiful - *and it was right there!*

The same applied to the other images. A friend, saying something nice to me… And yes, there was a bit of a wrong motive there, not even known to my friend himself. I had noticed it, I had stopped there, and with a superior smile I had classified his words in the drawer marked « Don't believe them ». But why had I stopped there? For, looking through my guide's glasses, I suddenly saw more. I saw a bit of real friendship there, a real core, a real care. But disdainfully I had shrugged it off, because it was not as ideal as I had wished it to be.

Another sob shook me, from the top of my head right down to my toes.

I saw myself then. I saw my own, what I had cynically called, « vain » efforts to love. I heard a hateful voice say, 'It's all show anyway. You know very well you can't love. You don't have the right feelings.'
I felt a bit surprised. Why ever had I believed that voice? Who was talking there anyway? And by what right?
Because, like a glittering diamond hidden under the dirt, I could see real love in me.

On and on it went… I saw my faith.
Panic! 'Not right, not enough, not good enough, not real,' I heard myself saying. Yes, myself. Imitating that same cold voice, making it my own, adopting its accusations.

17) REFRAMING

There were pictures everywhere; small ones, huge ones, beautiful ones, ugly ones… They all had different frames. In fact, the frames attracted my attention first.

« Strange, » I said to my companion. « Normally the frames are there to serve the pictures. Here the opposite seems true. Look at that picture of the girl over there… its frame has such wild and strange colours that you can hardly concentrate on her… »

He nodded. « True. It's the wrong frame. She needs another. »

He continued to look thoughtfully at the picture. « Listen, » he said after a while. « Can you hear anything? »

I listened hard. « There are voices coming out of it, aren't there? »

Again he nodded. « The frame is alive. In fact, every frame you see here is alive, but most of them are out of order. They tell lies about the pictures, they don't do them justice. »

« Why not change them, then? » I ventured.

He smiled. « Why not change them, indeed? We're already busy on that. Sometimes it takes a long time though, because the picture itself has to agree. And if it doesn't want a change of frame... »

I sighed. « You seem to me awfully respectful around here. A bit too much for my taste. Remember the soul-plant for instance, why was the gardener so keen on having its permission to replant it? You said something like 'The law of the country demands it' - but frankly, why? Why not just force the good on someone, especially on someone ignorant? You said yourself that the frame doesn't suit the picture. But the picture doesn't seem to notice, otherwise it wouldn't refuse a replacement. So, why let it decide about something it can't even see? »

I was quite satisfied with this little speech, it sounded nice and coherent in my own ears.

« You mean, why don't we interfere more? Well, I'm afraid I can't tell you more than what I already told you. The laws of the country allow patience, persuasion, persever-ance… even a little push here and there, now and then. But they definitely forbid manip-ulating, imposing your will, and generally bullying around. I'll tell you why. Take that frame, for instance. »

He walked to the picture of the girl. « Listen to what it says. »

Coming closer I could hear the voice, or voices, quite clearly.

'Go away,' one of them said. I didn't know whether it was talking to the girl, to me or my guide. Or to all of us. 'We don't want you.'

I held my breath. The girl in the picture had moved at those words, it was as if she were shrinking.

While I was watching, the colours of the frame changed, and suddenly it produced a picture all by itself, enfolding the one of the girl. Right now the loud colours had faded out to a rather cold grey and brown. The voice sounded cold, too, and horribly indifferent. 'You can just die, you know,' it went on, 'we won't miss you. Nobody will miss you. In fact, I wonder if they'll even notice.'

The girl nodded. She was pale, and too meagre. Still, she looked nice, and I felt a burst of anger shooting through me.

The voice droned on, 'I think you can just about give up. You're all alone, all by yourself, and nobody will ever take your defense. So, what's the use of going on? Why fight? What for?'

The girl hung her head.

That was enough. Before I knew what I was doing I lunged forward and started to batter the frame with my fists, trying to break it away from the picture. To my great satisfaction I heard a tearing noise. Wildly I plucked at the frame again, trying to sever it completely from the girl, but I only partly succeeded. The broken pieces hung crazily down, but stuck to the picture in a way that was beyond me.

Defiantly I looked over my shoulder at my companion. « Help me! » I shouted. But he was talking to the girl. « He's right, you know, » he told her very gently. « This is not the right frame for you, it doesn't suit you, for you were neither made with it nor for it. Will you not let it go? »

The girl looked anxious. « But isn't the voice right? » she asked. « Isn't that what reality is all about? I think you mean well, and I thank you for that, but I'd rather stick to it. It is so well in tune with what I live through every day, it seems very true to me. »

Meanwhile I was standing there, breathing hard, my hands hanging limply down. I felt perplexed.

« How *can* you believe it? » I asked. « How could such a horrible cold clammy *stupid* voice say the truth about you? Stop it! Don't believe it any more! »

« What else can I believe? » the girl asked sadly, but stubbornly. « All the frame-pictures say the same. »

Helplessly, I looked at the guide.

Still watching the girl intently, he answered, « It's because it started so early. It was one of the first things she heard, so she mistook it for the truth. She thinks she belongs to it and that it belongs to her. »

As if to confirm these words, the frame-picture changed again. I saw an old man bending over a little baby. His face was a little indifferent, but not unfriendly.

'This one's not going to live,' he stated, shrugging his shoulders.

I was surprised to find myself on the verge of tears. « What can we do? Please... I won't leave her here like that! »

« Of course you won't! » said my friend. « Let's go for it together! I'll stop the pieces that you broke off from coming together again. You see how they do? And you... well, you do whatever you think is right. »

I looked at him doubtfully. Whatever could I do? But he was already embracing the picture right there where the frame struggled to put itself back into place, putting himself between the two of them, all the time looking expectantly at me, so I didn't have much choice.

Remembering what he had said about not forcing things, even less people, remembering also the gentle ways of the lady with the children, I asked the girl,

« Can I come closer? »

She hesitated, then nodded. The fear in her eyes made my heart ache. « Shall I... shall I put my arm around your shoulder? Only as long as you want, » I added hastily, when I saw her eyes widen.

Again she nodded. I even thought I heard her say, « Please », but I wasn't sure.

It was strange to see the frame from the inside. Suddenly there were a lot of people crowding in on us, making a lot of noise, filling all the space. They were laughing, confident. Some of them were reading their Bibles and saying what seemed to me coldly correct and horrible things, ignoring the fact that they were trampling all over the girl. I got so terribly angry then, I just flung my fist in the face of one of them, who looked ever so surprised, but backed away nevertheless, taking the others with him.

For how long we stood there, the guide and I, holding the girl and murmuring nice words into her ears, I don't know. She didn't respond much, but I felt it was the right thing to do, and I didn't mind, oh, I didn't mind at all… It was as if some old, deep longing in my own heart was touched and awakened.

At last, the girl heaved a deep sigh. « Thank you, » she said simply. « That helped a lot. »

I let her go, all the while keeping a watchful eye on the hateful frame.

She followed my look. « Yes, it's strange, isn't it? » she said. « At moments like these, I can see it for what it is, as alien. I want to shake myself clear of it, but it keeps sticking to me with some kind of magical glue… »

She turned to my friend, whom she seemed to know. « Why is it like that? » she asked. There was hurt in her voice. « Why is it not enough that we both want it to go? Even this man, » - a look in my direction - « seems to want it to disappear, and still it's there. You know how much I've tried. What do I do wrong? »

He looked at her, caressing her hand.

« You don't do anything wrong » he said, very gently. « Only, the time of complete healing has not come yet. But look at your frame. Do you see a difference? »

The girl and I both looked. The frame was wriggling to return to its original shape, but it clearly wasn't successful. There were holes in it, and the figures seemed more ghostlike than before.

« Yes, » she answered, « yes, I see. But I still think it's my fault. Somehow I can't find the right thing to do, the right thing to say… »

Immediately, the frame seemed to get a bit stronger, its colours brighter.

« Don't repeat the lies! » the guide said sharply. « Remember it's not the truth. Don't strengthen the illusion by believing it. »

The girl smiled, ruefully now. « How often you told me, » she said. « And again and again I let it fasten its grip on me. Thank you for coming to my rescue. You'll continue helping me, won't you? When you do... » - she hesitated, glancing at me - « ... bring your friend. He's nice. »

I started blabbing something incoherent like « Not at all!, » but I felt immensely pleased.

« We'll have to go now, » said my friend. « But you're not alone, remember? »

« What happened to her? » I blurted out, when we had walked for a minute or so.

« She got a curse - and she took it, » was his brief response.

« A *what*?! »

« A curse. Oh, not one of those lamentable dark, intentional, evil ones; they're even worse. No, this one was just clumsy. Somebody told the mother that this girl wouldn't live. Thinking of course, with this stupid ignorance people sometimes display, that the baby wouldn't understand. » He snorted. « As if it needed words to understand what he was talking about. Anyway, it was one of the first messages of her life, and she took it for *the* first, not being able to recognize it for what it was, a stupid off-hand remark. Not remembering the *very* first message that I whispered into her heart, even before she was born… »

I looked at him. « How come she didn't remember ? »

« Because my adversary was playing clever. He made some more distorted messages come through, which confirmed the clumsy one. Some things happened that, normally, would have been sorted out and even forgotten. But now they all shouted the same message, over and over again, 'No place for you!' She tried to make sense of it, and instead of blaming the people she started blaming herself. A little girl can hardly do otherwise… »

He was silent for a moment. Then he continued, « The nasty thing is that psychological wounds can have spiritual consequences… and vice-versa. In other words, the old man's remark gave the adversary a foothold, from where he tries to attack. Those words, unintentionally but effectively, have much the same shape and colour as a real curse, and so they can borrow the latter's qualities. That's why the frame is so strong… »

I thought I understood. « So that's why you insist all the time we should respect the person, and ask for permission? Being very careful not to repeat the wrong words, the wrong pattern? »

« Yes. Otherwise we become just another voice on the frame. And then we can't help her. For you can't break the frame by using its own voices. And you can't enter the picture through the wrong frame. Let's say, we don't like to do it that way, even if, from time to time, we have to. We know it's much more healing to create a wholly different frame, like we did today. If she wants, she can accept this new one, and get familiar with it. I know, it's a long way round… »

« But the shortest way home ? » I completed, a bit acidly.

« She will heal in the end, you know, » he said, putting a friendly hand on my shoulder.

« And yes, I do think it is the shortest way home. But I see you're not convinced. »

« I begin to see your point, » I said reluctantly. « But I have another question. Why did you say she wasn't alone? We just left her! »

He stopped, and looked me fully into the eyes. « Do you really think I left her? »

I didn't say anything.

« Why do you think she knew me? » he went on. « Or why, for that matter, do you think the others around here do? »

Still I remained silent.

« Trust me. Try to, at least. I'm as much, and totally, and concentratedly with her, *right now*, as I am with you. Do you believe me? »

And, with surprise and not a small amount of delight I discovered that, yes, I did.

*****

18) GOING ON

There were many other moments. Maybe I'll tell you about them one day… Maybe not.

But this is as far as the story goes.

I've tried to describe some important stages of this surprising journey, where I finally learned to see.

Strange. I remember feeling so sheepish, a bit offended even, when he told me he'd come to teach me just that… to see. And my reaction: « See? Me?! Well thank you, but I get on quite well without you…! »

Now I smile to myself when I think of that. I haven't come to the end of my journey yet, not by a long shot. But at least I know one thing now. I wasn't, am not, and will never be able to see on my own.

Oh yes, I can see all right.

But I cannot *SEE* !

Truth was hidden from my eyes, but now… well, now I see a little bit further.

And I'm not going to let go of my companion either. I'll stick to him for the rest of my life. No going back to dull, lifeless, lightless, colourless would-be-reality for me! Once you discover the real thing, you don't want anything less. No risk of going back to a moldy poster-copy when you've seen the real picture.

Then I laugh aloud. Give me the Original, any time!

My name is still Tim Jonas.

I still think it's a funny name.

And I'm still a bit of a loner, awkward in company, relationship-handicapped, so to speak.

But we're working on that.

Because I'm not alone any more.

Never *ever* alone any more…

****

Breinigsville, PA USA
10 March 2011
257367BV00001B/8/P